BUCOLIC COMEDIES

BUCOLIC COMEDIES

BY

EDITH SITWELL

DUCKWORTH & CO.

3 HENRIETTA STREET, COVENT GARDEN, LONDON

TO

ARNOLD BENNETT

WITH HOMAGE TO HIS ART,
AND IN GRATITUDE FOR HIS GENEROUS RECOGNITION
OF MY WORK AT A MOMENT WHEN SUCH ENCOURAGE-
MENT WAS RARE.

First published in 1923
All rights reserved

Printed in Great Britain by Butler & Tanner, *Frome and London*

CONTENTS

NINETEEN BUCOLIC POEMS   PAGE

    I   Early Spring 11
   II   Spring 12
  III   Aubade 14
  IV   Fox Trot 16
   V   Cacophany for Clarinet . . 18
  VI   Rose 20
 VII   Gardener Janus Catches a Naiad . 22
VIII   The Five Musicians . . . 23
  IX   The Higher Sensualism . . 25
   X   King Cophetua and the Beggar Maid . 27
  XI   Clown Argheb's Song . . . 28
 XII   Poor Martha 29
XIII   Fleecing Time 31
XIV   Country Dance 33
 XV   Evening 35
XVI   On the Vanity of Human Aspirations . 37
XVII   Green Geese 40
XVIII   Kitchen Song 42
XIX   Spinning Song 43

Why 45
The Toilette of Myrrhine . . . 47
En Famille 49

FAÇADE

    I   Père Amelot 52
   II   "The Wind's Bastinado" . . 53
  III   Lullaby for Jumbo . . . 55
  IV   Trio for Two Cats and a Trombone . 56
   V   "Dame Souris Trotte" . . 58
  VI   Dark Song 59
 VII   Fête Galante 60
VIII   The Owl 61
  IX   Alone 62

			PAGE
X	" Fading slow, and furred is the Snow "		63
XI	" Said King Pompey, the Emperor's Ape "		64
XII	"The Sky was of Cinnamon "	. .	65
XIII	Ass-Face.		66
XIV	"The Octogenarian leaned from his Window "		67
XV	" Said the Noctambulo " . . .		68
XVI	Herodiade's Flea		69
XVII	Water Party		70
XVIII	Hornpipe		71
XIX	Sir Belzebub		73

TWO PROMENADES SENTIMENTALES

I	Rain	74
II	The Professor Speaks	76

Winter	78
Herodiade	81
The Doll	82

SPLEEN

I	Platitudes	84
II	Fantoches	85
III	By the Lake	87
IV	Lady Immoraline	88
V	Fantasia for Mouth-Organ . . .	90

NOTE

I am indebted to the editors of *The Spectator*, *The Weekly Westminster Gazette*, *The English Review*, *Form*, *The Athenæum* and the Poetry Bookshop's *Monthly Chapbook* for permission to include some of these poems—others have already appeared in *Wheels*, and I have to thank the publishers, Messrs. Parsons, for permission to reprint; and some again have appeared in my privately printed book *Façade*, but many of the poems appearing under the heading " Façade " are new.

"I am a member of a race whose tradition is hunting (of the rare and the unattainable), whose skill in falconry was used indiscriminately on the smallest song-birds and on a winged and blinded Fate."—*An autobiography*. EDITH SITWELL.

"We are accused of triviality; but poetry is no longer a just and terrible Judgment Day—a world of remorseless and clear light. The poet's mind has become a central sense, interpreting and controlling the other five senses; for we have rediscovered the truth uttered by Blake, that 'Man has no body distinct from his soul, for that called body is a portion of soul discern'd by the five senses, the chief inlets of Soul in this age.' Modern poets are discovering an entirely new scale of relationship between the senses. Our senses have become broadened, and cosmopolitanized. They are no longer little islands, speaking only their own narrow language, living their sleepy life alone. Where the language of one sense is insufficient, they speak the language of another. We know, too, that every sight, touch, sound, smell, of the world we live in, has its meaning—is the result of a spiritual state (as a great philosopher said to me)—is, in short, a kind of psycho-analysis. And it is the poet's duty to interpret those meanings."
—*From an essay by* EDITH SITWELL.

"Heart-break is no longer the gigantic wreckage left from the combats of beasts and of gods, but a little and gradual change, melancholy and shallow as the withdrawal caused by the slow dropping of water

7

upon some vast stone image.   This slow withdrawal will change the tragic mask through which strange gods have cried, until, seen through the death-cold rents in the saturnine leaves, it seems, almost, to echo in its form the cold laughter of the water.   And this, too, is the fate of the comedy masks, smiling and clear as vermilion fruits.   Modern heart-break is merely a dulling and a retrogression, a travelling backward : till man is no longer the bastard of beasts and of gods, but is blind, eyeless, shapeless as the eternal stones, or exists with the half-sentience of the vegetable world —a sentience that is so intensely concerned with the material world (as apart from the visual) that it is like the sentience of the blind."—*From an essay by* EDITH SITWELL.

NINETEEN BUCOLIC POEMS

" COUNTRYSIDES where the people know that Destiny is befouled and has feathers like a hen . . . landscapes where the leaves have an animal fleshinesss, and old pig-snouted Darkness grunts and roots in the hovels. There, the country gentlemen are rooted in the mould ; and they know that beyond the sensual aspect of the sky (that harsh and goatish tent) something hides—but they have forgotten what it is. So they wander, aiming with their guns at mocking feathered creatures that have learnt the wonder and secret of movement, beneath clouds that are so low-hung that they seem nothing but wooden potting-sheds for the no-longer disastrous stars . . . (they will win the prize at the local flower-show). The water of the shallow lake gurgles like a stoat, murderously ; the little unfledged feathers of the foam have forgotten how to fly, and the country gentleman wanders, hunting for something—hunting ! "—*From an essay by* EDITH SITWELL.

Early Spring

THE wooden châlets of the cloud
    Hang down their dull blunt ropes to shroud

Red crystal bells upon each bough
(Fruit-buds that whimper). No winds slough

Our faces, furred with cold like red
Furred buds of satyr springs long dead !

The cold wind creaking in my blood
Seems part of it, as grain of wood ;

Among the coarse goat-locks of snow
Mamzelle still drags me to and fro ;

Her feet make marks like centaur hoofs
In hairy snow ; her cold reproofs

Die, and her strange eyes look oblique
As the slant crystal buds that creak.

If she could think me distant, she
In the snow's goat-locks certainly

Would try to milk those teats the buds
Of their warm sticky milk—the cuds

Of strange long-past fruit-hairy springs—
Beginnings of first earthy things !

Spring

To Helen

WHEN spring begins, the maids in flocks
  Walk in soft fields, and their sheepskin locks

Fall shadowless, soft as music, round
Their jonquil eyelids, and reach the ground.

Where the small fruit-buds begin to harden
Into sweet tunes in the palace garden

They peck at the fruit-buds' hairy herds
With their lips like the gentle bills of birds.

 . . . . . .

But King Midas heard the swan-bosomed sky
Say " All is surface and so must die."

And he said : " It is spring ; I will have a feast
To woo eternity ; for my least

Palace is like a berg of ice ;
And the spring winds for birds of paradise

With the leaping goat-footed waterfalls cold
Shall be served for me on a dish of gold

By a maiden fair as an almond-tree,
With hair like the waterfalls' goat-locks ; she

Has lips like that jangling harsh pink rain,
The flower-bells that spirt on the trees again."

In Midas' garden the simple flowers
Laugh, and the tulips are bright as the showers,

For spring is here ; the auriculas
And Emily-coloured primulas

Bob in their pinafores on the grass
As they watch the gardener's daughter pass.

Then King Midas said " At last I feel
Eternity conquered beneath my heel

Like the glittering snake of Paradise—
And you are my Eve ! "—but the maiden flies

Like the leaping goat-footed waterfalls
Singing their cold, forlorn madrigals.

Aubade

J ANE, Jane,
     Tall as a crane,
        The morning light creaks down again.

Comb your cockscomb-ragged hair ;
Jane, Jane, come down the stair.

Each dull blunt wooden stalactite
Of rain creaks, hardened by the light,

Sounding like an overtone
From some lonely world unknown.

But the creaking empty light
Will never harden into sight,

Will never penetrate your brain
With overtones like the blunt rain.

The light would show (if it could harden)
Eternities of kitchen garden,

Cockscomb flowers that none will pluck,
And wooden flowers that 'gin to cluck.

In the kitchen you must light
Flames as staring, red and white

As carrots or as turnips, shining
Where the cold dawn light lies whining.

Cockscomb hair on the cold wind
Hangs limp, turns the milk's weak mind. . . .

     Jane, Jane,
     Tall as a crane,
     The morning light creaks down again !

Fox Trot

O^{LD} Sir
Faulk,
Tall as a stork,
Before the honeyed fruits of dawn were ripe, would
walk
And stalk with a gun
The reynard-coloured sun
Among the pheasant-feathered corn the unicorn has
torn, forlorn the
Smock-faced sheep
Sit
And
Sleep,
Periwigged as William and Mary, weep . . .
" Sally, Mary, Mattie, what's the matter, why cry ? "
The huntsman and the reynard-coloured sun and I
sigh
" Oh, the nursery-maid Meg
With a leg like a peg
Chased the feathered dreams like hens and when they
laid an egg
In the sheepskin
Meadows
Where
The serene King James would steer
Horse and hounds, then he
From the shade of a tree

Picked it up as spoil to boil for nursery tea," said the
      mourners.   In the
Corn, towers strain
Feathered tall as a crane,
And whistling down the feathered rain, old Noah
      goes again—
An old dull mome
With a head like a pome,
Seeing the world as a bare egg
Laid by the feathered air ; Meg
Would beg three of these
For the nursery teas
Of Japhet, Shem, and Ham ; she gave it
Underneath the trees
Where the boiling
              Water
              Hissed
Like the goose-king's feathered daughter—kissed
Pot and pan and copper kettle
Put upon their proper mettle
Lest the Flood begin again through these !

Cacophany for Clarinet

SAID the dairymaid
      With her hooped petticoat
Swishing like water . . .
To the hemlocks she said, " Afraid
Am I of each sheep and goat—
For I am Pan's daughter ! "
Dark as Africa and Asia
The vast trees weep—
The Margravine learned as Aspasia,
Has fallen asleep.
Her small head, beribboned
With her yellow satin hair
Like satin ribbons butter-yellow
That the faunal noon has made more mellow
Has drooped asleep . . .
And a snore forlorn
Sounds like Pan's horn.
On pointed toe I creep—
Look through the diamonded pane
Of the window in the dairy,—
Then out I slip again
In my hooped petticoat like old Morgane the fairy.
Like a still-room maid's yellow print gown
Are the glazed chintz buttercups of summer
Where the kingly cock in a feathered smock and a
      red-gold crown

Rants like a barn-door mummer.
And I heard the Margravine say

To the ancient bewigged Abbé
" I think it is so clever
Of people to discover
New planets—and how ever
Do they find out what their names are ? "
Then, clear as the note of a clarinet, her hair
Called Pan across the fields, Pan like the forlorn wind,
From the Asian, African darkness of the trees in his
      lair,—
To play with her endless vacancy of mind !

VI

Rose

(Imitated from Skelton)

IN the fields like an Indian mazery
 That the foolish moon has flowered,
Rose Bertin is walking lazily where
The fringe of the field is bowered

With trees as dark as the ancient creeds
Of China and of Ind . . .
Rose Bertin walks through the fields' pearled weeds
Where haunts the satyr wind.

"Where are you going to, my pretty maid,"
That negroid satyr sighs . . .
"To feed my pretty chucks, sir," she said—
"Each feathered thing that flies."

To feed them with the sun's gold grains
In the fields' sparse Indian chintz ;
But now those grains are spilt like rains
But still light feathery glints

Fly in my brain . . . those bright birds flock :
The butterbump, the urban
Ranee stork, the turkey-cock
(Red paladin in a turban),

The crane who talks through his long nose,
The plump and foolish quail—
In their feathered robes they follow Rose,
And never once they fail.

And Harriet, Susan, Rose, and Polly,
Silken and frilled as a pigeon
Sleek them and praise the golden folly
That made laughing Rose a religion.

Gardener Janus Catches a Naiad

BASKETS of ripe fruit in air
   The bird-songs seem, suspended where

Between the hairy leaves trills dew
All tasting of fresh green anew.

Ma'am, I've heard your laughter flare
Through your waspish-gilded hair :

     Feathered masks,
     Pots of peas,
     Janus asks
     Nought of these,
     Creaking water
     Brightly stripèd
     Now I've caught her—
     Shrieking biped.
     Flute sounds jump
     And turn together,
     Changing clumps
     Of glassy feather.
     In among the
     Pots of peas
     Naiad changes—
     Quick as these.

VIII

The Five Musicians

To Osbert

THE blue-leaved fig-trees swell with laughter,
   Gold fissures split the ripe fruits after,

And like a gold-barred tiger, shade
Leaps in the darkness that they made.

The long-ribbed leaves shed light that dapples
Silenus like a tun of apples;

Gold-freckled, fruit-shaped faces stare
At nymphs with bodies white as air.

The ancient house rocked emptily
" Horned brothers, creep inside and see

Through my tall windows : the abode
Of noise is on the dusty road."

They creep . . . strange hands are on the hasp . . .
Silenus, sleepy as a wasp

Amid the fruit-ripe heat as in
An apricot or nectarine

Replies, " The dust is wise and old . . .
For glistening fruits and Ophir's gold

Are gathered there to wake again
In our flesh, like a tune's refrain."

The five musicians with their bray
Shatter the fruit-ripe heat of day ;

Their faces, wrinkled, kind, and old
Are masked by the hot sun with gold ;

Like fountains of blue water, gush
Their beards. Strange-feathered birds that hush

Their song, move not so proud as these
Smiles floating, ageless courtesies.

They stand upon the dust outside ;
Their tunes like drops of water died.

Yet still we hear their slow refrain,
" King Pharaoh, gay lad, come again ! "

Miss Nettybun, beneath the tree,
Perceives that it is time for tea

And takes the child, a muslined moon,
Through the lustrous leaves of afternoon.

And tea-time comes with strawberry
Jam—yet where, oh *where*, is she ?

On that music floating, gone
To China and to Babylon ;

Never again she'll go to bed
In the house of Sir Rotherham Redde !

24

The Higher Sensualism

QUEEN CIRCE, the farmer's wife at the Fair,
    Met three sailor-men stumping there,

Who came from the parrot-plumed sea, Yeo-Ho !
And each his own trumpet began to blow.

"We come," said they, "from the Indian seas,
All bright as a parrot's feathers, and these

Break on gold sands of the perfumed isles,
Where the fruit is soft as a siren's smiles,

And the sun is as black as a Nubian.
We singed the beard of the King of Spain. . . .

Then we wandered once more on the South Sea strand
Where the icebergs seem Heavenly Mansions fanned

By the softest winds from the groves of spice,
And the angels like birds of paradise

Flit : there we caught this queer-plumaged boy
(An angel, he calls himself) for a toy."

    .   .   .   .

The Angel sighed : "Please, ma'am, if you'll spare
Me a trumpet, the angels will come to the Fair ;

For even an angel must have his fling,
And ride on the roundabout, in the swing ! "

She gave him a trumpet, but never a blare
Reached the angels from Midsummer Fair,

Though he played, " Will you hear a Spanish lady ? "
And " Jack the Sailor," " Sweet Nelly," " Trees
    shady "—

For only the gay hosannas of flowers
Sound, loud as brass bands, in those heavenly bowers.

Queen Circe said, " Young man, I will buy
Your plumaged coat for my pig to try—

Then with angels he'll go a-dancing hence
From sensuality into sense ! "

The Fair's tunes like cherries and apricots
Ripened ; the angels danced from their green grots ;

Their hair was curled like the fruit on the trees . . .
Rigaudon, sarabande, danced they these.

And the pig points his toe and he curves his wings,
The music starts and away he flings—

Dancing with angels all in a round,
Hornpipe and rigaudon on the Fair's ground.

King Cophetua and the Beggar Maid

To Alan Porter

THE five-pointed crude pink tinsel star
    Laughed loudly at King Cophetua ;

Across the plain as black as mind
And limitless, it laughed unkind

To see him whitened like a clown
With the moon's flour, come in a golden crown.

The moon shone softer than a peach
Upon the round leaves in its reach ;

The dark air sparkled like a sea—
The beggar-maid leaned out through a tree

And sighed (that pink flower-spike full of honey),
" Oh, for Love ragged as Time, with no money ! "

Then through the black night the gardener's boy
As sunburnt as hay, came whispering, " Troy

Long ago was as sweet as the honey-chimes
In the flower-bells jangling into rhymes,

And, oh, my heart's sweet as a honey-hive
Because of a wandering maid, and I live

But to tend the pale flower-bells of the skies
That shall drop down their dew on her sleeping eyes."

Clown Argheb's Song

CLOWN Argheb the honey-bee
Counted his money, "See
In the bandstand in Hell,
Buzzing, the tunes that fell
Raise up glass houses, round
Serres chaudes as forcing-ground
Lest bald heads harden
In Hell's kitchen garden."
Poet and pedagogue
Bump their bald heads agog—
(Melon and marrow,
And cucumber narrow.)
Next day comes Proserpine,
Parasol raised, and "See,
Ma'am," says the gardener, "these
Thoughts are as thick as peas!"
So sighed the clown, singing
Buzz, and still clinging,
To no horizontal bars,
But the pink freezing stars!

Poor Martha

BY white wool houses thick with sleep
    Wherein pig-snouted small winds creep,

With our white muslin faces clean,
We slip to see what can be seen.

Those rustling corn-sheaves the gold stars
Drop grain between the window-bars

Among dark leaves all velvety—
(So seem the shadows) and we see

Crazed Martha tie up her brown hair
With the moon's blue ribbons, stare

At candles that are lit in vain—
They cannot penetrate her brain :

Their tinsel jargon seems to be
Incomprehensibility

To Martha's mind, though every word
Of hers they echo, like that bird

Of brilliant plumage, whose words please
The Indians by their bright-plumed seas.

The Fair's tunes bloom like myosotis
Smooth-perfumèd stephanotis ;

We children come with twisted curls
Like golden corn-sheaves or fat pearls,

Like ondines in blue muslin dance
Around her ; never once a glance

She gives us : "Can my love be true ?
He promised he would bring me blue

Ribbons to tie up my brown hair.
He promised me both smooth and fair

That he would dive through brightest plumes
Of Indian seas for pearls, where glooms

The moon's blue ray ; in her sleeping-chamber
Find me Thetis' fan of amber."

. . . .

The candles preen and sleek their feathers . . .
"Pretty lady !" "Sweet June weathers."

But silence now lies all around
Poor Martha, since her love is drowned.

Fleecing Time

QUEEN VENUS, like a bunch of roses,
Fat and pink, that splashed dew closes,

Underneath dark mulberry trees,
Wandered with the fair-haired breeze.

Among the dark leaves, preening wings,
Sit golden birds of light ; each sings,

" Will you accept the blue muslin ? "
As they peck the blackamoor mulberries' skin.

Then came a sheep like a sparkling cloud ;
" Oh ma'am, please ma'am, sleek me proud,

Come fleece and comb my golden wool
And do not mind, ma'am, if you pull ! "

Her flocks came thick as the mulberries
That grow on the dark, clear mulberry trees,

As thick as the daisies in the sky . . .
Prince Paris, Adonis ; as each passed by

She cried, " Come feed on buds as cold
As my fleeced lamb-tailed river's gold,

And you shall dance like each golden bird
Of light that sings in dark trees unheard,

And you shall skip like my lamb-tailed river,
In my buttercup fields for ever."

The lady Venus, with hair thick as wool,
Cried " Come and be fleeced—each sheepish fool ! "

Country Dance

THAT hobnailed goblin, the bob-tailed Hob,
   Said " It is time I began to rob."
For strawberries bob, hob-nob with the pearls
Of cream (like the curls of the dairy girls),
And flushed with the heat and fruitish-ripe
Are the gowns of the maids who dance to the pipe.
Chase a maid ?
She's afraid !
" Go gather a bob-cherry kiss from a tree,
But don't, I prithee, come bothering me ! "
She said—
As she fled.
The snouted satyrs drink clouted cream
'Neath the chestnut-trees as thick as a dream ;
So I went
And leant
Where none but the doltish coltish wind
Nuzzled my hand for what it could find.
As it neighed,
I said,
" Don't touch me, sir, don't touch me, I say,
You'll tumble my strawberries into the hay."
Those snow-mounds of silver that bee the spring
Has sucked his sweetness from, I will bring
With fair-haired plants and with apples chill
For the great god Pan's high altar . . . I'll spill
Not one !
So in fun

We rolled on the grass and began to run
Chasing that gaudy satyr the Sun.
Over the haycocks, away we ran
Crying " Here be berries as sunburnt as Pan ! "
But Silenus
Has seen us. . . .
He runs like the rough satyr Sun.

Come away !

XV

Evening

PRINCE ABSOLAM and Sir Rotherham Redde
Rock on a rocking-horse home to bed

With dreams like cherries ripening big
Beneath the frondage of each wig.

In a flat field on the road to Sleep
They ride together, a-hunting sheep

That like the swan-bright fountains seem ;
Their tails hang down as meek as a dream.

Prince Absolam seems a long-fleeced bush,
The heat's tabernacle, in the hush

And the glamour of eve, when buds the dew
Into bright tales that never come true ;

And as he passes a cherry-tree
Caught by his long hair, bound is he,

While all his gold fleece flows like water
Into the lap of Sir Rotherham's daughter.

Come then, and sit upon the grass
With cherries to pelt you, as bright as glass—

Vermilion bells that sound as clear
As the bright swans whose sighing you hear

When they float to their crystal death
Of water, scarcely plumed by the breath

Of air—so clear in the round leaves
They look, this crystal sound scarce grieves

As they pelt down like tears fall'n bright
From music or some deep delight.

The gardener cut off his beard of bast
And tied up the fountain-tree, made it fast

And bound it together till who could see
Which is Prince Absolam, which is the tree?

Only his gold fleece flows like water
Into the lap of Sir Rotherham's daughter;

Sir Rotherham Redde gathers bags of gold
Instead of the cherries ruddy and cold.

On the Vanity of Human Aspirations

"In the time of King James I, the aged Countess of
Desmond met her death, at the age of a hundred and forty
years, through falling from an apple-tree."—*Chronicles of the
times*.

IN the cold wind, towers grind round,
   Turning, turning, on the ground.

In among the plains of corn
Each tower seems a unicorn.

Beneath a sad umbrageous tree
Anne, the goose-girl, could I see—

But the umbrageous tree behind
Ne'er cast a shadow on her mind—

A goose-round breast she had, goose-brains,
And a nose longer than a crane's;

A clarinet sound, cold, forlorn,
Her harsh hair, straight as yellow corn,

And her eyes were round, inane
As the blue pebbles of the rain.

Young Anne, the goose-girl, said to me,
"There's been a sad catastrophe!

The aged Countess still could walk
At a hundred and forty years, could talk,

And every eve in the crystal cool
Would walk by the side of the clear fish-pool.

But to-day when the Countess took her walk
Beneath the apple-trees, from their stalk

The apples fell like the red-gold crown
Of those kings that the Countess had lived down,

And they fell into the crystal pool ;
The grandmother fish enjoying the cool—

(Like the bright queens dyed on a playing-card
They seemed as they fanned themselves, flat and hard),—

Floated in long and chequered gowns
And darting searched for the red-gold crowns

In the Castles drownèd long ago
Where the empty years pass weedy-slow

And the water is flat as equality
That reigns over all in the heavenly

State we aspire to, where none can choose
Which is the goose-girl, which is the goose . . .

But the Countess climbed up the apple-tree,
Only to see what she could see—

Because to persons of her rank
The usual standpoint is that of the bank ! . . ."

The goose-girl smoothed down her feather-soft
Breast . . . "When the Countess came aloft,

King James and his courtiers, dressed in smocks,
Rode by a-hunting the red-gold fox,

And King James, who was giving the view-halloo
Across the corn, too loudly blew,

And the next that happened was—what did I see
But the Countess fall'n from the family tree!

Yet King James could only see it was naughty
To aspire to the high at a hundred and forty,

'Though if' (as he said) 'she aspired to climb
To Heaven—she certainly has, this time!'"

. . . And Anne, the goose-girl, laughed, "Tee-hee,
It was a sad catastrophe!"

Green Geese

To Richard Jennings

THE trees were hissing like green geese . . .
    The words they tried to say were these :

" When the great Queen Claude was dead
They buried her deep in the potting-shed."

The moon smelt sweet as nutmeg-root
On the ripe peach-trees' leaves and fruit,

And her sandal-wood body leans upright,
To the gardener's fright, through the summer night.

   .   .   .   .   .

The bee-wing'd warm afternoon light roves
Gilding her hair (wooden nutmegs and cloves),

And the gardener plants his seedsman's samples
Where no unicorn herd tramples—

In the clouds' potting-sheds he pots
The budding planets in leaves cool as grots,

For the great Queen Claude when the light's gilded
    gaud
Sings Miserere, Gloria, Laud.

But when he passes the potting-shed,
Fawning upon him comes the dead—

Each cupboard's wooden skeleton
Is a towel-horse when the clock strikes one.

And light is high—yet with ghosts it winces
All night 'mid wrinkled tarnished quinces,

When the dark air seems soft down
Of the wandering owl brown.

They know the clock-faced sun and moon
Must wrinkle like the quinces soon

(That once in dark blue grass dew-dabbled
Lay) . . . those ghosts like turkeys gabbled

To the scullion baking the Castle bread—
"The Spirit too, must be fed, be fed ;

Without our flesh we cannot see—
Oh, give us back Stupidity ! " . . .

But death had twisted their thin speech
It could not fit the mind's small niche—

Upon the warm blue grass outside,
They realized that they had died.

Only the light from their wooden curls roves
Like the sweet smell of nutmegs and cloves

Buried deep in the potting-shed,
Sighed those green geese, " Now the Queen is dead."

Kitchen Song

THE harsh bray and hollow
    Of the pot and the pan
Seems Midas defying
The great god Apollo !
The leaves' great golden crowns
Hang on the trees ;
The maids in their long gowns
Hunt me through these.
Grand'am, Grand'am,
From the pan I am
Flying . . . country gentlemen
Took flying Psyche for a hen
And aimed at her ; then turned a gun
On harmless chicken me—for fun.
The beggars' dogs howl all together,
Their tails turn to a ragged feather ;
Pools like mirrors hung in garrets
Show each face as red as a parrot's
Whistling hair that raises ire
In cocks and hens in the kitchen fire !
Every flame shrieks cockle-doo-doo
(With their cockscombs flaring high too) ;
The witch's rag-rug takes its flight
Beneath the willows' watery light :
The wells of water seem a-plume—
The old witch sweeps them with her broom—
All are chasing chicken me. . . .
But Psyche—where, oh where, is she ?

Spinning Song

THE miller's daughter
    Combs her hair,
Like flocks of doves
As soft as vair . . .

Oh, how those soft flocks flutter down
Over the empty grassy town.

    Like a queen in a crown
    Of gold light, she
    Sits 'neath the shadows'
    Flickering tree—

Till the old dame went the way she came,
Playing bobcherry with a candle-flame.

    Now Min the cat
    With her white velvet gloves
    Watches where sat
    The mouse with her loves—

(Old and malicious Mrs. Grundy
Whose washing-day is from Monday to Monday.)

    "Not a crumb," said Min,
    "To a mouse I'll be giving,
    For a mouse must spin
    To earn her living."

So poor Mrs. Mouse and her three cross Aunts
Nibble snow that rustles like gold wheat plants.

And the miller's daughter
Combs her locks,
Like running water
Those dove-soft flocks ;

And her mouth is sweet as a honey-flower cold
But her heart is heavy as bags of gold.

The shadow-mice said
" We will line with down
From those doves, our bed
And our slippers and gown,

For everything comes to the shadows at last
If the spinning-wheel Time move slow or fast."

To Sacheverell

NOAH'S granddaughter
    Sat on his knee ;
Her questions like water
Gushed ceaselessly.

Her hair's gilded wool
Seems the sun's tent ;
Her mouth, a grape golden-cool,
Shows through the rent.

Noah's replies
Are all one hears ;
And the small ripples rise
Like listening ass-ears.

" That young giraffe ?
His proud elevation
Raises a laugh
To the height of quotation. . . .

The camel's face
Is like Mrs. Grundy's ;
He makes that grimace
At working on Sundays. . . .

The kangaroo, chaste,
Of Victorian complexion,
Wears at her waist
Each pledge of affection.

The trunk of the elephant
Is not a box,
The cock's gilded crown can't
Frighten the fox."

. . . . .

The sea-gods talk Greek . . .
But they learn the word " why ";
Like leaves of the palm
Their beards gilded and dry

Are spreading upon
The blue marble Pompeii
Whose temples are gone
(So the sea seems) ; Aglae

Asks " What for ? " . . . The waves' door
Begins to slam.
Like water the questions pour.
Noah said " Damn ! "

SIESTA time is hot in Hell !
    Down the glittering shutters fell
With a noise Arabian
Like the rustling pearls that fan

The eyes of rajahs when they hide
Beyond the incense-flowing tide
Their majesty, all lonely save
For the hot Nubian sun, their slave.

And like the lovely light gazelles
Walking by deep water-wells,
Shadows past her mirrors fleet
Through bright trellises of heat.

Through the shutters fawning crept
A barber zephyr, cringing stept
Through the shutters fallen like water—
Hiding Hell's most lovely daughter.

The sun, a ripened apricot,
Still made the flattened roof-tops hot,
And at her table preened and set
Myrrhine sits at her toilette.

" Madame Myrrhine, if you please,"
Fawning said the barber breeze,
" I will coiff as light as air
That Arabian wind your hair."

Never had the perfumed seas
Such bright grape-black curls as these

Fallen like rustling pearls that run,
Burnt by the hot Nubian sun,

From each elephantine trunk
The waterfalls rear. Myrrhine shrunk,
But now the barber zephyr curls
Black cornucopias of pearls.

Upon the dressing-table, heat
Is flaunting like a parokeet,
And in the street dust-white and lean,
Two black apes bear her palanquin.

Through the shutters see those apes'
Eyes like green and golden grapes . . .
Their falsetto voices made
A false simian serenade.

The negress Dinah through unheard
Shutters like the sun's gold gourd
Bears her powder-puff—the breath
Of an angel, a swan's death.

Never once Myrrhine replies
To those apes with slanting eyes . . .
She died a thousand years ago—
From dust her beauty ripened slow.

But Fanfreluche her parrot closes
With the ballerina roses—
Pecks them—Dinah longs to snatch
The night to make her beauty-patch.

En Famille

IN the spring-time, after their tea,
Through the fields of the springing Bohea,
Jemima, Jocasta, Dinah, and Deb
Walked with their father Sir Joshua Jebb—
An admiral red whose only notion
(A butterfly poised on a pigtailed ocean)
Is of the peruked sea whose swell
Breaks on the flowerless rocks of Hell.
Under the thin trees Deb and Dinah,
Jemima, Jocasta, walked, and finer
Their black hair seemed (flat-sleek to see)
Than the leaves of the springing Bohea ;
Their cheeks were like nutmeg-flowers when swells
The rain into foolish silver bells.
They said, " If the door you would only slam,
Or if, Papa, you would once say ' Damn '—
Instead of merely roaring ' Avast '
Or boldly invoking the nautical Blast—
We should now stand in the street of Hell
Watching siesta shutters that fell
With a noise like amber softly sliding ;
Our moon-like glances through these gliding
Would see at her table preened and set
Myrrhina sitting at her toilette
With eyelids closed as soft as the breeze
That flows from gold flowers on the incense-trees."

.　　.　　.　　.　　.　　.　　.

The Admiral said, " You could never call—
I assure you it would not do at all !

She gets down from table without saying ' Please,'
Forgets her prayers and to cross her T's,
In short, her scandalous reputation
Has shocked the whole of the Hellish nation ;
And every turbaned Chinoiserie
With whom we should sip our black Bohea
Would stretch out her simian fingers thin
To scratch you, my dears, like a mandoline ;
For Hell is just as properly proper
As Greenwich or as Bath or Joppa ! ''

FAÇADE

"This modern world is but a thin match-board flooring spread over a shallow hell. For Dante's hell has faded, is dead. Hell is no vastness; there are no more devils who laugh or who weep—only the maimed dwarfs of this life, terrible straining mechanisms, crouching in trivial sands, and laughing at the giants' crumbling!"—*An essay.* EDITH SITWELL.

FAÇADE

I

Père Amelot

THE stars like quaking-grass grow in each gap
    Of air (ruined castle wall) . . .
Père Amelot in his white nightcap
Peered through . . . saw nothing at all.

Like statues green from the verdigris
Of the moon, two shadows join
His shade, that under that castle wall sees
The moon like a Roman coin.

Out of his nightcap he drew three pence . . .
Marie and Angélique pass
The knife through Père Amelot's back—in the dense
Bushes fly . . . he nods on the grass.

The man with the lanthorn a moment after
Picks up the moon that fell
Like an Augustan coin when laughter
Shook the hen-cackling grass of Hell.

And the Public Writer inscribing his runes
Beneath that castle wall, sees
Three Roman coins as blackened as prunes—
And Père Amelot slain for these !

The stars like quaking-grass grow in each gap
Of air—ruined castle wall . . .
Père Amelot nods in his white nightcap . . .
He knows there is nothing at all !

II

THE wind's bastinado
        Whipt on the calico
Skin of the Macaroon
And the black Picaroon
Beneath the galloon
Of the midnight sky.
Came the great Soldan
In his sedan
Floating his fan,—
Saw what the sly
Shadow's cocoon
In the barracoon
Held.   Out they fly.
" This melon,
Sir Mammon,
Comes out of Babylon :
Buy for a patacoon—
Sir, you must buy ! "
Said Il Magnifico
Pulling a fico,—
With a stoccado
And a gambado
Making a wry
Face : " This corraceous
Round orchidaceous
Laceous porraceous
Fruit is a lie !
It is my friend King Pharaoh's head
That nodding blew out of the Pyramid. . . ."

. . . The tree's small corinths
Were hard as jacinths
For it is winter and cold winds sigh . . .
No nightingale
In her farthingale
Of bunchèd leaves let her singing die.

III

Lullaby for Jumbo

JUMBO asleep !
   Grey leaves thick-furred
As his ears, keep
Conversations blurred.
Thicker than hide
Is the trumpeting water ;
Don Pasquito's bride
And his youngest daughter
Watch the leaves
Elephantine grey :
What is it grieves
In the torrid day ?
Is it the animal
World that snores
Harsh and inimical
In sleepy pores ?—
And why should the spined flowers
Red as a soldier
Make Don Pasquito
Seem still mouldier ?

IV

Trio for Two Cats and a Trombone

L ONG steel grass—
    The white soldiers pass—
The light is braying like an ass.
See
The tall Spanish jade
With hair black as nightshade
Worn as a cockade !
Flee
Her eyes' gasconade
And her gown's parade
(As stiff as a brigade).
Tee-hee !
The hard and braying light
Is zebra'd black and white
It will take away the slight
And free
Tinge of the mouth-organ sound
(Oyster-stall notes) oozing round
Her flounces as they sweep the ground.
The
Trumpet and the drum
And the martial cornet come
To make the people dumb—
But we
Won't wait for sly-foot night
(Moonlight, watered milk-white, bright)
To make clear the declaration
Of our Paphian vocation

Beside the castanetted sea
Where stalks Il Capitaneo
Swaggart braggadocio
Sword and moustachio—
He
Is green as a cassada
And his hair is an armada.
To the jade " Come kiss me harder "
He called across the battlements as she
Heard our voices thin and shrill
As the steely grasses' thrill
Or the sound of the onycha
When the phoca has the pica
In the palace of the Queen Chinee !

V

" Dame Souris trotte
gris dans le noir."

MADAME MOUSE trots
Grey in the black night !
Madame Mouse trots :
Furred is the light.
The elephant-trunks
Trumpet from the sea . . .
Grey in the black night
The mouse trots free.
Hoarse as a dog's bark
The heavy leaves are furled . . .
The cat's in his cradle,
All's well with the world !

VI

Dark Song

THE fire was furry as a bear
    And the flames purr. . . .
The brown bear rambles in his chain [1]
Captive to cruel men
Through the dark and hairy wood . . .
The maid sighed, " All my blood
Is animal. They thought I sat
Like a household cat ;
But through the dark woods rambled I . . .
Oh, if my blood would die ! "
The fire had a bear's fur
It heard and knew . . .
The dark earth furry as a bear,
Grumbled too !

[1] This line and the two following lines came into my
mind through hearing a song of Stravinski's. I do not know its
name and I only heard it once ; but it contained lines rather
like these.

VII

Fête Galante

IN the muscadine-glowing noon
    Under the arcade
Shaped like a cascade—
Where the shadows creep like a pantaloon—
The Abbé finished his rhodomontade.
" Madame la Marquise,
If you please,
When I must play with old ladies, ombre
In Hades' shady bocage sombre—
Let me, though I am old,
Still perceive your gold
Fruit-sweet cheeks' brocade,
Smiling among that peaceful shade. . . ."
But the Marquise in the bocage,
Laughs like the sharp rockage
Of her gallant grottoes, cold as water-wells,
And shakes her curls, as pearly as their shells !

VIII

The Owl

THE currants moonlit as Mother Bunch
    In their thick-bustled leaves were laughing like
    Punch ;
And, ruched as their country waterfalls,
The cherried maids walk beneath the dark walls.
Where the moonlight was falling thick as curd
Through the cherry-branches, half-unheard
Said old Mrs. Bunch, the crop-eared owl,
To her gossip : " If once I begin to howl,
I am sure that my sobs would drown the seas—
With my ' oh's,' and my ' ah's,' and my ' oh dear
    me's ! '
Everything wrong from cradle to grave—
No money to spend, no money to save ! "
And the currant-bush began to rustle
As poor Mrs. Bunch arranged her bustle.

IX

Alone

THE vast grey trees
    Float on the breeze—
Strings of grey pearls float
Vaguely from these,
And the Countess calls
To her two Pekinese—
(Korin's grey waterfalls—
Wave-like Chinoiseries).
Oh, this long avenue
Reaches for ever ! . . .
" Are you still true
Though our lives dissever ? "
The empty wind with the cat's voice sang
To the sun as strange as the Admiral Yang,
Whose face is as flat as the notes
Of pianolas ; whose hair is like black frigate boats,—
There is nothing to give
And nothing to buy—
It is too late to live
And too late to die,
Since the sad spring came again
With its red lacquer buds and its pain,
And that chapeau chinois [1]
The frizzed wind blew
(Piquant minois)
In the long avenue !

[1] A seventeenth-century court instrument.

X

FADING slow
　　And furred is the snow
As the almond's sweet husk,
And smelling like musk.
The snow amygdaline
Under the eglantine
Where bristling stars shine
Like a gilt porcupine—
The snow confesses
The little Princesses
On their small chioppines
Dance under the orpines.
See the casuistries
Of their slant flutt'ring eyes—
Gilt as the zodiac
(Dancing herodiac).
Only the snow slides
Like gilded myrrh
From the rose-branches—hides
Rose-roots that stir !

XI

SAID King Pompey, the emperor's ape,
  Shuddering black in his temporal cape
Of dust : " The dust is everything—
The heart to love and the voice to sing,
Indianapolis,
And the Acropolis,
Also the hairy sky that we
Take for a coverlet comfortably." . . .
Said the Bishop
Eating his ketchup—
" There still remains Eternity
(Swelling the diocese)—
That elephantiasis
The flunkeyed and trumpeting Sea ! "

XII

THE sky was of cinnamon,
    Stars were like cloves. . . .
The wind cherubinical
Fawning and finical,
Faintly inimical,
Wears silken gloves.
Came the great palanquin—
Slowly it passes
Over the dull
Chain-armour grasses
Where the shadow-hounds bark
In a pack, in the park,
And the sea-urchin sighs
With a small sad din
"What finds the winter wind
Hiding within?"
The Great Mogul
Whose face like a camel
Looks with disdain
At each smaller mammal!
But, this Bank Holiday,
Little brittle girls
Toss at this ghost their gay
Cinnamon curls!
"Though one cannot go far
Because of the seas'
Black horsehair sofa—
Yet on the breeze
Each wave like a soldier
Stiffly advances,
Asking the mouldier
Maids for dances!"

A SS-face drank
  The asses' milk of the stars . . .
The milky spirals as they sank
From heaven's saloons and golden bars,
Made a gown
For Columbine,
Spirting down
On sands divine
By the asses' hide of the sea
(With each tide braying free).
And the beavers building Babel
Beneath each tree's thin beard,
Said " Is it Cain and Abel
Fighting again we heard ? "
It is Ass-face, Ass-face,
Drunk on the milk of the stars,
Who will spoil their houses of white lace—
Expelled from the golden bars !

XIV

THE octogenarian
    Leaned from his window,
To the valerian
Growing below
Said " My nightcap
Is only the gap
In the trembling thorn
Where the mild unicorn
With the little Infanta
Danced the lavolta
(Clapping hands : molto
Lent' eleganta)."
The man with the lanthorn
Peers high and low ;
No more
Than a snore
As he walks to and fro. . . .
Il Dottore the stoic
Culls silver herb
Beneath the superb
Vast moon azoic.

XV

BENEATH the gilt capricorn
  Said the Noctambulo
Turning his folio
To the papillio
By the night born :
" I nod my head
And the great Avatar
With his scented guitar
And his scimitar,
Pretends to be dead.
And my snore forlorn
Is a horn
That will blow
Down the gilt capricorn
And the walled Jericho."

XVI

CAME the great Popinjay
    Smelling his nosegay :
In cages like grots
The birds sang gavottes.
" Herodiade's flea
Was named sweet Amanda,
She danced like a lady
From here to Uganda.
Oh, what a dance was there !
Long-haired, the candle
Salome-like tossed her hair
To a dance-tune by Handel " . . .
Dance they still ?   Then came
Courtier Death,
Blew out the candle-flame
With civet breath.

XVII

Water Party

R OSE Castles
  Those bustles
Beneath parasols seen !
Fat blondine pearls
Rondine curls
Seem. Bannerols sheen
The brave tartan
Waves' Spartan
Domes—(Crystal Palaces)
Where like fallacies
Die the calices
Of the water-flowers green.
Said the Dean
To the Queen
On the tartan wave seen :
" Each chilly
White lily
Has her own crinoline,
And the seraphs recline
On divans divine
In a smooth seventh heaven of polished pitch-pine."
Castellated,
Related
To castles the waves lean
Balmoral-like ;
They quarrel, strike
(As round as a rondine)
With sharp towers
The water-flowers

And, floating between,
Each chatelaine
In the battle slain—
Laid low by the Ondine.

XVIII

Hornpipe

SAILORS come
    To the drum
Out of Babylon ;
    Hobby-horses
Foam, the dumb
Sky rhinoceros-glum

Watched the courses of the breakers' rocking-horses
    and with Glaucis,
Lady Venus on the settee of the horsehair sea !
Where Lord Tennyson in laurels wrote a gloria free
In a borealic iceberg came Victoria ; she
Knew Prince Albert's tall memorial took the colours
    of the floreal
And the borealic iceberg ; floating on they see
New-arisen Madam Venus for whose sake from far
Came the fat and zebra'd emperor from Zanzibar
Where like golden bouquets lay far Asia, Africa,
    Cathay,
All laid before that shady lady by the fibroid Shah.
Captain Fracasse stout as any water-butt came, stood
With Sir Bacchus both a-drinking the black tarr'd
    grapes' blood

Plucked among the tartan leafage
By the furry wind whose grief age
Could not wither—like a squirrel with a gold star-nut.
Queen Victoria sitting shocked upon the rocking-horse
Of a wave said to the Laureate, " This minx of course
Is as sharp as any lynx and blacker-deeper than the
     drinks and quite as
Hot as any hottentot, without remorse !

            For the minx,"
                      Said she,.
        " And the drinks,
                  You can see

Are hot as any hottentot and not the goods for me ! "

XIX

WHEN
    Sir
Belzebub called for his syllabub in the hotel in Hell

    Where Proserpine first fell,

Blue as the gendarmerie were the waves of the sea

    (Rocking and shocking the bar-maid).

Nobody comes to give him his rum but the
Rim of the sky hippopotamus-glum
Enhances the chances to bless with a benison
Alfred Lord Tennyson crossing the bar laid
With cold vegetation from pale deputations
Of temperance workers (all signed In Memoriam)
Hoping with glory to trip up the Laureate's feet

    (Moving in classical metres) . . .

Like Balaclava, the lava came down from the
Roof, and the sea's blue wooden gendarmerie
Took them in charge while Beelzebub roared for his
    rum.
        . . . None of them come !

TWO PROMENADES SENTIMEN-TALES

I

Rain

BESIDE the smooth black lacquer sea
You and I move aimlessly.

The grass is springing pale, alone,
Tuneless as a quartertone. . . .

Remote your face seems, far away
Beneath the ghostly water, Day,

That laps across you, rustling loud—
Until you seem a muslined cloud

Beneath your fluted hat's ghost-flowers—
The little dog that runs and cowers

Black as Beelzebub, now tries
To catch the white lace butterflies. . . .

But we are mute and move again
Across the wide and endless plain,

Vague as the little nachreous breeze
That plays with gilt rococo seas.

We are two ghosts to-day—each ghost
For ever wandering and lost ;

No yesterday and no to-morrow
Know we—neither joy nor sorrow,

For this is the hour when like a swan
The silence floats, so still and wan

That bird-songs, silver masks to hide
Strange faces now all sounds have died,

Find but one curdled sheepskin flower
Embodied in this ghostly hour. . . .

II

(The Professor speaks)

ONE time when the cold red winter sun
    Like a Punch and Judy show shrilled in fun

And scattered down its green perfume
Like the dust that drifts from the green lime-bloom,

I sat at my dressing-table—that chilly
Palely crinolined water-lily

And watched my face as spined and brittle
As the tall fish, tangled in a little

Dark weed, that sea-captains keep
In bottles and perpetual sleep.

My face seemed the King of Spain's dry map
All seamed with gold . . . no one cared a rap

As I walked on the grass, like the sheepish buds
Of wool that grow on lambs chewing their cuds.

The small flowers grew to a hairy husk
That holds Eternity for its musk

And the satyr's daughter came : I saw
She was golden as Venus' castle of straw,

And the curls round her golden fruit-face shine
Like black ivy-berries that will not make wine.

76

With my black cloak—(a three-tiered ship on the main)
And my face like the map of the King of Spain,

Beneath the boughs where like ragged goose-plumes
Of the snow hang the spring's first chilly blooms,

I swept on towards her ; my foot with the gout
Clattered like satyr-hoofs, put her to rout,

For she thought that I was the satyr-king . . .
So she fled like the goat-legged wind of spring

Across the sea that was green as grass,
Where bird-soft archipelagos pass—

To where like golden bouquets lay
Asia, Africa and Cathay.

And now the bird-soft light and shade
Touches me not ; I promenade

Where rain falls with tinkling notes and cold
Like the castanet-sound of the thinnest gold

In chessboard gardens where, knight and pawn
Of ivory, scentless flowers are born.

To Veronica

DAGOBERT lay in front of the fire . . .
    Each thin flame seemed a feathery spire

Of the grasses that like goslings quack
On the castle walls : " Bring Gargotte back " ;

But Gargotte the goose-girl, bright as hail,
Has faded into a fairy-tale.

The kings and queens on the nursery wall
Seem chain-armoured fish in the moat, and all

The frost-flowers upon the window-panes,
Grown fertilate from the fire's gold grains,

Ripen to gold-freckled strawberries,
Raspberries, glassy-pale gooseberries—

(We never could touch them, early or late,
They would chill our hands like the touch of Fate).

But Anne was five years old and must know
Reality ; in the goose-soft snow

She was made to walk with her three tall aunts
Drooping beneath the snow's cold plants.

They dread the hour when with book and bell
Their mother, the old fell Countess of L——

Is disrobed of her wig and embalmed for the night's
Sweet mummified dark ; her invective affrights

78

The maids till you hear them scamper like mice
In the wainscoting—trembling, neat and nice.

Each clustered bouquet of the snows is
Like stephanotis and white roses;

The muted airs sing Palestrina
In trees like monstrances, grown leaner

Than she is; the unripe snow falls
Like little tunes on the virginals

Whose sound is bright, unripe and sour
As small fruits fall'n before their hour.

The Countess sits and plays fantan
Beneath the portrait of great Queen Anne

(Who sleeps beneath the strawberry bed);
And all her maids have scampered, fled.

The shuffled cards like the tail of a bird
Unfolding its shining plumes are heard. . . .

The maid in her powder-closet soon
Beneath the fire of the calm full moon

Whose sparkles, rubies, sapphires spill
For her upon the window-sill

Will nod her head, grown sleepy, I wis,
As Alaciel or Semiramis,

Pasiphae or the lady Isis,
Embalmed in the precious airs like spices.

But her ladyship stamps with her stick . . . " Grown
   cold
Are my small feet, from my chilly gold—

Unwarmed by buds of the lamb's wool . . . go
And gather for me the soft polar snow

To line with that silver chilly-sweet
The little slippers upon my feet—

With snow clear-petalled as lemon blossom—
Crystal-clear—perfumed as Venus' bosom."

. . . .

Can this be Eternity ?—snow-peach-cold,
Sleeping and rising and growing old

While she lies embalmed in the fire's gold sheen
Like a cross wasp in a ripe nectarine,

And the golden seed of the fire droops dead
And ripens not in the heart or head !

To Inez

THE snow dies, that was cold as coral
    Or a fairy-story's moral,

And birds put forth their song's soft flowers
In the thickets and the bowers.

Salome walks the lands . . . the quaint
Flowers crisp as snow, and youthful, feint

To watch from Heaven's palaces,
With footsteps soft as calices

The angels came as pages, show
Salome how to touch the low

Lute-notes and dance the sarabande,
Leading the Princess by the hand,

Until Salome's nurse appears,
Harsh as the snow ; with shivering fears

The angels go again, discern
Theirs is no dance that she must learn.

The Doll

IF cold grew visible again,
    We should see bell-flowers on the plain

With shivering stalks, as white as kings
In trembling ermine. Each one rings

A little tune for vespers, matins,
Beneath the polar sky's red satins;

(The cold is but the shivering
Of the white flower-bells as they ring.)

And Madame A . . . the elegante,
With Madame X, the elephant,

Walked down the lengthy avenue
Carrying their missals; and they knew

The point-lace hanging from the trees
Delicately laughed at these,

Knowing they'd find no angels there
With their apple-curling hair

Because the angels pulled the lapel
Of the priest's robe, left the chapel,

And with my doll and me in Heaven
Hear the nursery clock strike seven.

The angels and myself between us
We break their doll the lady Venus

Whose curls seem petalled orange-flowers
From Heaven's tree (those perfumed showers

Fall like soft music in the mind).
Seeing my doll they are unkind

To all their toys ; they break with joy
The bird-soft bricks that builded Troy—

Laugh at the thought that it could matter.
The angels' feet like bird-feet patter

Across the floor ; they leave their needle
Sticking in their samplers, wheedle

Me to let them wash my daughter
Until her face is clear as water,

Her curls like bell-flowers one can see
At Easter, jangling on a tree.

. . . .

But nurse is wandering on the plain,
'Midst cold grown visible again ;

She looks for me, and as she walks
On toes the cold has turned to stalks

'Mid shrill steel grasses that dissemble
The cold (bell-flowers that jangle, tremble)

The angels nod their small heads, say
" It's time we were in bed, stopped play " . . .

Yet still the angels overhead
Play with my doll, though I'm in bed !

SPLEEN

I

Platitudes

THE news of Queen Anne's death comes to arouse
The Dead, in the quilted red satin house

Where the country gentlemen from their birth
Like kind red strawberries root in earth.

Then weeping come the dairy girls
With their ivy curls and their cheeks like pearls;

They leave the cheese and they leave the milk
That Pan will steal—it is white as silk.

Peruked waves curl and break a splinter
From the flat pearled shore of winter

And candle-flames bob like strawberries low
Over the thick and cream-like snow;

While the dairy girls weep; "Who cares," they said,
"If old and cross Queen Anne be dead?"

They wept, "She lies in her palace chamber
Embalmed in the cold like a wasp in amber

While a fawning courtier-like air roves
In among the dark shadow-groves. . . .

And dead is our faun who loved the sheen
Of the snow that is cold as a nectarine!"

II

Fantoches

THE stars were like prunes . . .
　　Wrinkled, the winter breeze.
In nightgowns buffoons
Wrote dusty lampoons.
"Where is Sir Plato
And where is Queen Anne?
Forgotten like Cato!
Less than a man
Is now that disaster
The mage Zoroaster
Who could not survive our runes, our lampoons,
Withered as stars that are darker than prunes!"
. . . Blown along in her palanquin
Tattered and thin,
In her quilted red satin,
Miss Pekoe reads Latin.
Like sequins
From Pekin's
Treasuries these
Eyes of Miss Pekoe;
Illogicalisms
Her limbs, and an echo
Her face; syllogisms
Her hat.　Astronomical
Trees where swoons
The breeze, hide coxcomical
Lanthorn moons
Set in the trees

Like bird-lime.
The third time,
An old buffoon croons
To a fluttering moth :
" Dust is the cloth
That made Cleopatra
And every peninsular
House ; dark Sumatra,
Miss Pekoe grown insular,
The saturnine asinine bray of the seas ! "

III

By the Lake

A CROSS the thick and the pastel snow
   Two people go. . . . " And do you re-
   member
When last we wandered this shore ? " . . . " Ah no !
For it is cold-hearted December."

" Dead, the leaves that like asses' ears hung on the trees
When last we wandered and squandered joy here ;
Now Midas your husband will listen for these
Whispers—these tears for joy's bier."

And as they walk, they seem tall pagodas ;
And all the ropes let down from the cloud
Ring the hard cold bell-buds upon the trees—codas
Of overtones, ecstasies, grown for love's shroud.

IV

Lady Immoraline

To the Memory of Robert Ross

FROM the great house platformed flat as a cage
    Above the clouds' widened landing-stage,
We watch the carriages driving home
By the goggling and gilded dragons of foam.

"Beautiful carriages from Champs Elysée
Filled with fair maidens on cushions easy" [1]
Drive by the gilt Second Empire sand
Where leaves of black gauze enliven the band.

    "Do you remember
      Semiramis,
      Bright as September? . . .
      Gone is her kiss. . . ."

Said Lady Immoraline . . . old is she
As a mummy. She sipped her black bohea
With Sir Horace Walpole, the Emperor Nero
And that old general, Cæsar the hero.

The lovely lotus buds of the snow
Bloom into brightness, fading slow :
And now she drives, all shrunken and old
By the sea and the sands' Second Empire gold

---

[1] These two lines, by Georgina Farrer, were quoted by
Mr. Ross as an example of the worst poetry.

Where the spray seems like wheat-ears
And Ethiopias'
Fruits—cornucopias
For beauty's bier.

V

Fantasia for Mouth-Organ

" I HAD a mother-in-
Law ; no other kin
Could be so kind," said
He !
"She worried till the bladder
Of my figure seemed a ladder,
And wrangled till she cancelled it. She
Would wring me on the mangle
When the hot sun's jangle
Bent the North Pole to South, and
The
Wind hyperborean
Dried the marmorean
Wash for a nominal
Fee.
But the wheezing wind's harmonium
Seemed an encomium
Of life when one is
Free,
And as life was getting barrener
I set out as a mariner—
The hero of this epopee.
I sailed on botanic
Gardens oceanic
Where siren-birds sip Bohea—
Past the lodging-houses lean
Where like oozing glycerine
The ozone drips ; and the wee

Horses age had tattered
Flap along the battered
Platform grasses (green as tea),
But the ship and the narrator
Had traversed the equator
Before I knew that Fate's decree
Had seen fit to decide
The mother of my bride
To companion the refugee !
The South Pole floating past
Was taller than a mast—
The North Pole and the South congree
O'er the ocean of red horsehair
(Unknown of any corsair)
In the snow's cold ivory—
All smooth as a japonica,
In sound like an harmonica,
Where the humming-bird quick lights flee
To the polar sea's pavilion.
We paid for twenty million
Red velvet drinks with one rupee,
And in the central hulk
My mother-in-law's bulk
Sat reared upon the snow's settee.
Her jangling jet bonnet
(With the polar lights upon it)
A cathedral seemed, whose key
Was her nose, a horny cockatrice
Goggling out to mock at these
Sights ; for every degree
Of the North Pole and the South
Had for bonnet, seas uncouth—

Electric fish a-curl like a trochee
Are their lithe and writhing locks.
The redskins came in flocks
And pelted hairy fruitage from the tree.
Then we floated back toward
The equator ; flat as sward,
And green as grass the water seemed to be.
Like a dulcimer or zither
Was the tinkling and the glitter
Of the icebergs as they floated aerily.
For on water soft as calices
That open, Crystal Palaces
Were those bergs of ice ; within their apogee
Were the queerest, brightest pictures—
Exhibitions with the strictures
Vanished from the Infinite ; and we
Then traversed the equator.
And it was either Fate or
Whatever other power is our pawnee—
But when natives with smooth joints
And features like gilt points
Of the starfish moon came dancing a boree,—
Their eyes like wrinkled tortoises
And their hair's black vortices
Whirled, as they sunk upon one
Knee.
For when they saw
My mother-in-law
They decided not to tackle
Me !
She is tough as the armorian
Leather that the saurian

Sun spreads over the
Sea—
So she saved my life,
Did the mother of my wife—
Who is more than a mother to
Me !"

"We all remember nursery afternoons when the snow's little old musical-box gave out half-forgotten tunes, and our nurse told us tales that fell with the same tinkling notes as the snow's tunes. . . . 'Long ago, and once upon a time.' But though this world has the same bright-coloured clarity as those afternoons of our childhood, it is a different world. The snow lies cold to our heart. Here we have a winter world, stripped bare of all its smiling leaves, and the soul is face to face with reality."—

An essay. EDITH SITWELL.

REVIEWS

"A great many, though not all, of the best works of art in every kind are a little ' difficult ' to the hearer or the reader.

"To say that it is well worth the reader's while to persevere with the obscurer poems of Miss Sitwell and to try to understand them is, I sometimes feel, the only part of the critic's function which I can properly fulfil in regard to her.

"The Sitwells' work is really extraordinarily odd. At first reading it often seems merely superficially inconsequent. The disturbing thing is that at second reading it seems logical, but with an inapplicable sort of logic. The Sitwells live in a spiritual and emotional fourth-dimensional space. There is somewhere some small deflection of the stream of consciousness which has taken them to a new and often most attractive world."—A. WILLIAMS ELLIS in *The Spectator*.

"Valery Larbaud once astonished and delighted me by stating, quite on his own, that the most accomplished of all the younger British poets was Edith Sitwell ; a true saying, though I had said it before him."—ARNOLD BENNETT in an article on " Ulysses " in *The Outlook*.

"As a composer of fantastical verse Miss Sitwell is fully aware of her own limitations. This is only another way of saying that she is a first-class writer.

"If after reading the following lines ('Herodiade ') you disagree with me, I recommend you to wait thirty years and peruse the poem in Sir Joshua Jebb's Anthology (published in 1951). You will then be safe to enjoy it automatically, unless you have passed into coffin or crematorium. . . . I am not surprised that anthologists are still busily and brusquely boycotting Miss Sitwell. Anthologists usually compile conventionally ; rabidly they reject anything unforeseen. ' What would Coleridge say to such asylum-stuff ? ' ejaculates some exasperated gentleman, flinging ' Façade ' on the floor.

Question.

' What would Mr. Coleridge say
In Nineteen Twenty-Two ? '

Answer.

' Miss Edith Sitwell's verses ought to be
Admired for their originality.'

Chorus.

' And that's what Coleridge says to you
In good old Nineteen Twenty-Two.'

95

"Probably Mr. C. would add that Miss S. writes for her own ears and sees with her own eyes, which is a rare and exquisite achievement. The results are, of course, totally unexpected. To the intolerant and purblind the results are all 'damned nonsense.' All fantastic art is 'nonsense' until we have got over our astonishment. Miss Sitwell's originality has affinities with Aubrey Beardsley.

"'But Beardsley was an obscene artist!' shrieks some fat-headed critic of Miss Sitwell's 'asylum poetry.' The answer is that Aubrey was a great artist, and, as such, has triumphed over all the fat-heads of his day.

"Miss Sitwell will do the same."—SIEGFRIED SASSOON in *The Daily Herald*.

"With the Sitwell family . . . the dreaded name conjures up painful memories of being brought sharp up against an actually living attempt to express a new realization of loveliness. The result is confusing to the critic and even a little shocking, because beauty is like death in this, that you cannot have it at second hand. . . .

"Either in the presence of new beauty, one must accept it, a little breathlessly, or we must reject it from the system with drugs. The latter is the easier and the more general course adopted with the Sitwells. The Pan-British 'Pharmacopœia' is ransacked for suitable purgatives and anodynes against this almost incurable disease of beauty. The most modern method of inoculating it with its own germ, not being available to the critics, they must use the old poisons handed down from Dr. Johnson and the old Edinburgh. Here are the drugs : 'Impenetrable obscurity.' 'Fantastic avoidance of meaning.' 'Bravura that conceals all absence of art.' 'Impertinence.'—H. W. in a full-page essay on Sacheverell Sitwell, in the *Weekly Westminster Gazette*.

"Her vision and her technique are so individual as to be inimitable. Her manner of expression is admirably suited to herself; it is perhaps suited to nobody else."—EDWARD MOORE in *The New Age*.

"Miss Sitwell's perversity, ceasing to be ethical, has passed into the æsthetic perfection. She is indeed quite a virtuoso."—*The Times Literary Supplement*.

"We see her work at its best and most characteristic—the hallucinated vision, the precise glassily bright technique, the curiously profound wit, in the 'Fifteen Bucolic Poems.'"[1]—*Athenæum*.

[1] *These are not the "Bucolic Poems" included in this book, but an earlier set of poems.*

Panope

How lovely are the tombs of the dead nymphs
On the heroic shore—the glittering plinths
Of jacynth . . . hyacinthine waves profound
Sigh of the beauty out of sight and sound

And many a golden foot that pressed the sand—
Panope walking like the pomp of waves
With plumaged helmet near the fountain caves
The panoply of suns on distant strand—

Is only now an arena for the worm,
Her golden flesh lies in the dust's frail storm

And beauty water-bright for long is laid
Deep in the empire of eternal shade—

Only the sighing waves know now the plinth
Of those deep tombs that were of hyacinth.

But still the echoes of that helmeted bright hair
Are like the pomp of tropic suns, the blare

That from the inaccessible horizon runs—
The eternal music of heroic suns
When their strong youth comes freshened from deep seas—
And the first music heard among the trees.

                                        EDITH SITWELL.

New Republic

22 : 2 : 28

power, supplying 153,000,000 units of electricity to factories, farms and homes. Another ten million dollars will give us twice this capacity, and there are other streams besides the Shannon suitable for power development. The Shannon project"—it is clearly the apple of his eye—"will not only provide industrial power; it will bring comfort to the little homes that are now dark and cheerless on winter nights, and it will help stop the drift from the farms to the city slums. It will be, moreover, a solvent of political intransigeance.

"We have nationalized education. Under whatever economic pressure, the government intends to find money to educate every child and to foster such cultural activities as the Abbey Theater and the publication of Gaelic texts. As to objections to compulsory study of Gaelic, we do not think it necessary to defend the fostering of our national language. Experience shows it is good for the children; and modern business and affairs can be carried on in it without difficulty.

"We regret that Northern Ireland has not joined us, but we hope in time they will find it to their interest to do so. We live in perfect harmony with the North, and we do not forget that it was there the modern movement toward Irish independence